Religious Topics

INITIATION RITES

Jon Mayled

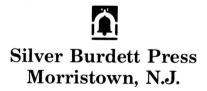

Silver Burdett Press
Morristown, N.J.

Religious Topics

Birth Customs   Initiation Rites
Death Customs   Marriage Customs
Feasting and Fasting   Pilgrimage

Cover *A Buddhist initiation ceremony in Thailand.*

First published in 1986 by Wayland (Publishers) Limited
61 Western Road, Hove, East Sussex, BH3 1JD England

© Copyright 1986 Wayland (Publishers) Limited

Adapted and first published in the United States in 1987 by
Silver Burdett Press, Morristown, New Jersey
Library of Congress Cataloging-in-Publication Data

Mayled, Jon.
    Initiation rites.

    (Religious topics)
    Bibliography: p.
    Includes index.
    Summary: Describes the customs in Buddhism,
Christianity, Hinduism, Judaism, and other
religions used to introduce people into the
religion as full members, usually held for young
people who are reaching adulthood.
    1. Initiation rites – Religious aspects –
Comparative studies – Juvenile literature.
[1. Initiation rites – Religious aspects]
I. Title.   II. Series.
BL615.M36   1987   291.3′8   86–31402
ISBN 0–382–09452–2

Phototypeset by Kalligraphics Limited, Redhill, Surrey, England
Printed in Italy by G. Canale & C.S.p.A., Turin

Contents

Introduction

One of the most important events in many people's religious lives is the ceremony of initiation. To be initiated is to be introduced into something. Many religions have special initiation ceremonies during which people are introduced into the religion as full members.

The Jewish Bar Mitzvah initiation ceremony. The ceremony of initiation is an important event in many people's religious lives.

Usually these ceremonies are held for young people who are reaching adulthood. When they were babies they were considered to be too young to make their own commitment. But now as they approach adulthood, they are considered to be old enough to take responsibility for their own religious lives.

During initiation ceremonies the people being initiated often make promises to their God and to the other members of their religion. Sometimes these ceremonies also include some kind of test. The priest or minister may ask the initiates questions about their religion. If they answer correctly, they prove that they are worthy of full membership in their religious group.

After initiation, the initiates are accepted as full members of their religion and can take part in many of the ceremonies and responsibilities of their faith.

Buddhist monks in Thailand. In Buddhism, initiation takes place when a person becomes a monk.

Buddhism

In Buddhism, initiation takes place only when a person becomes a monk. Many young men become monks, and now some women, too, are being prepared to be admitted as members of the *Sangha*, the order of monks.

After initiation the monks go to live in a Buddhist monastery, where they lead a holy

Young Buddhists in Sri Lanka dressed as princes before initiation.

life and study the *Dharma* (the teaching of the Buddha).

Most initiates stay in the monastery for just three months, but some stay for several years, and a few devote their whole lives to being monks.

Buddhist initiation ceremonies vary from one country to another. In Thailand, where many people follow a form of Buddhism called *Theravada*, a young man is helped to prepare for initiation by a *thera bikku*, someone who has been a monk for at least ten years. The initiate must also get permission from his employer and, if he is married, from his wife. Before the ceremony the young man's parents shave his head, then he is washed and dressed in white.

A procession of musicians and dancers then leads him to the monastery. There he chants his request to be ordained (to be made a monk). He then changes into yellow clothes

In Thailand, the heads of the young men are shaved before the initiation ceremony takes place.

Buddhist initiation ceremonies are often colorful.

and, after taking ten vows, the monks ordain him as a novice (beginner).

Next, the young man is questioned by the monks to make sure that he is suitable to become a monk. When they are satisfied,

Novice monks carrying alms bowls.

he is accepted and takes an additional 227 vows. He then gives flowers and gifts to the other monks. His own family and friends give him the few things he will need while he is at the monastery. These may include robes, sandals, tea, an umbrella, incense, candles, and an alms bowl (a dish in which the monks collect food and gifts from local people).

While he is in the monastery, the young man will lead a simple life, studying and praying. In this way, he learns about his religion before returning to his ordinary life outside the monastery.

Chinese

A Chinese family. The naming ceremony is an important religious event.

Chinese people who follow the Taoist religion do not have one single initiation ceremony. The main ceremony in Chinese people's religious lives take place when they are given their name. That is the beginning of their gradual initiation into the all-important family.

Chinese families are organized into large groups called clans, and the family members are very close to one another. As children grow older, they are given more and more duties within the clan and its religious life. This affects boys more than girls.

To some Chinese people, children are not considered "safe" until they are seven. This is because it is thought the influence of the stars and planets on them is still unstable. This dangerous time before the age of seven is called *m-saam, m-sz*, meaning "not three and

not four." After this age, children can play a full part in the life of the clan.

As the children grow into adulthood, they are gradually given more and more responsibilities. They are expected to take up a particular place in the clan and to obey the clan's wishes.

As Chinese children grow older, they play a larger part in the religious life of the clan.

Christianity

Most Christian babies are baptized when they are a few weeks old. At that time, specially-chosen adults, called godparents, make promises that they will bring the children up to believe in God and in Jesus.

When the children are older, they have to make their own commitment to Christianity. To become adult members of the Christian Church, they undergo initiation rites, called Confirmation. This means that the person confirms his or her belief in God and Jesus.

Confirmation usually takes place when people are between the ages of eleven and sixteen. Young people who wish to be Confirmed are called "candidates" and they go to special classes to make sure that they understand what they are doing and what their Confirmation means. Children can receive this teaching at their church.

In the Christian religion, most babies are baptized when they are a few weeks old.

12

The Confirmation service takes place in a church or other place of worship. During the service, candidates promise to try to live a

The Christian initiation rite of Confirmation.

A group of young girls dressed for their first Holy Communion ceremony.

Christian life and to follow the teachings of Christianity. A bishop lays his hands on the head of each person and welcomes them into the church congregation by name. This act is very important because the "laying on of hands" by bishops is a tradition that goes back in an unbroken line to Jesus and the disciples.

After the service, a party is usually held to celebrate the fact that the young person is a full member of the Christian community.

14

In some Christian churches, people have to be Confirmed before they can share in Holy Communion. This is the religious ceremony in which people share the bread and wine that Christians take together in church to remind them of the Last Supper, which Jesus ate with his disciples. Holy Communion takes place at a service called the Eucharist, or Mass.

In some Christian churches, people have to be Confirmed before they can share in Holy Communion.

15

The Hindu gods Vishnu (left), Brahma (middle above), and Shiva (right).

Hinduism

Hindus pass through sixteen stages in their lives. Each stage is dedicated to God by a ritual called a *samskara*. The first nine *samskaras* have to do with birth; the tenth, the initiation ceremony, is the most important of all. This is the *Upanayana*, or "sacred thread," ceremony. This *samskara* is only for boys. There is no similar ceremony for girls.

The ceremony, which takes place when a boy is between eight and twelve years of age, means that he is now ready to be taught about his religion from a guru, or teacher.

The boy's head is shaved for his new life and a thread made of three strands is placed over his shoulder. The thread reaches down to the opposite hip. The strands are sometimes made of grass, sometimes of the strings of a bow, and sometimes of wool. Which of these is used depends on how important the boy's family is.

The strands are tied together by a knot called the *brahma granthi*, or spiritual knot. No one is quite sure why there are three strands. Some think they may represent the three most important Hindu gods: Shiva, Vishnu, and Brahma.

After being given the thread, the boy receives a staff, or stick, which shows that he

The "sacred thread" ceremony is only for boys.

is now a student. The boy's guru will teach him the prayers that he is expected to say every day.

After the ceremony, the boy has a ritual bath to mark the start of his new life. Now he can be called a *snataka*, which literally means someone who has bathed.

In the past the boy would then leave his family and go away to study with his guru for twelve years. But this is no longer done. Instead the boy says goodbye to his mother, leaves the house, makes a brief symbolic journey, and returns home.

Islam

When a baby is born into a Muslim family, it automatically becomes a member of the Islamic faith. There are no special initiation ceremonies. Later, when young people are old enough to be treated as adults, they are expected to decide for themselves about following their religion.

However, some ceremonies have developed to mark various stages in a child's religious

There are no special initiation ceremonies in the Islamic faith.

19

An important part of the religious education of every Muslim child is to learn parts of the Qur'an.

development. Muslims in India have a ceremony called *Bismallah*, which takes place when a child is four years and four days old. The family's friends and relatives come to the house and the father teaches his child this phrase:

"Bismallah – hir – Rahman – nir – Rahmin"

This means:

"In the name of Allah the most gracious, the most merciful."

After this the child is taught some verses from the Muslim holy book, the *Qur'an*. At the end of the ceremony, sweetmeats are given to the guests.

When Muslim children are seven years old, they begin to receive their full religious education. Their parents teach them how to pray, showing them the positions in which to stand

and kneel. The children also learn to keep the fasts of Islam. These are the special days when they do not eat. An important part of their education is to learn parts of the *Qur'an* by heart.

By the time children are twelve or thirteen, they are expected to carry out their religious duties in the same way as adult Muslims.

Muslims at prayer. When Muslim children reach the age of seven, they are taught how to pray.

Judaism

When a Jewish boy becomes thirteen, and a Jewish girl becomes twelve, they are thought of as adults. They are then old enough to understand the *mitzvot*, the commandments and duties of being an adult Jew.

On the first Sabbath (Saturday) after a boy's thirteenth birthday, he attends an initiation ceremony called a *Bar Mitzvah* which means "a son of the commandments."

The boy goes to the synagogue and begins by saying a special prayer in which he promises God that he will:

> *"Keep Your commandments, and undertake and bear the responsibility of my actions towards You."*

The boy wears his prayer shawl (*tallit*) for the first time and performs his duty as an

On the first Sabbath after his thirteenth birthday, a Jewish boy will attend a Bar Mitzvah ceremony.

A Bat Mitzvah *ceremony at a synagogue in Sydney, Australia.*

adult Jew by reading out loud part of the *Torah*, the Jewish holy book. He will have practiced this for a long time before the ceremony, as the scrolls on which the *Torah* is written are in the Hebrew language.

After he has finished reading, the scrolls are replaced in the Ark, the receptacle in which they are kept. The rabbi now gives a talk, offering advice to the young boy about his life. This ends with a blessing:

> *"The Lord bless you, and keep you:*
> *The Lord makes his face to shine upon you,*
> *   and be gracious to you:*
> *The Lord lift up his face to you, and give*
> *   you peace."*

After the service, wine is blessed and food is served for everyone to celebrate. There are often other parties and celebrations over the weekend and the boy will receive presents, such as books, pens, and money.

In recent years, a similar service for girls has started among some Jews. This is called a *Bat Mitzvah*, which means "a daughter of the commandments." It usually takes place on the Sunday after the girl's twelfth birthday, when she recites a special prayer in the synagogue.

After the initiation service, everyone celebrates.

Sikhism

The most important event in the religious life of this young Sikh will be the initiation ceremony into the Khalsa.

For Sikhs, the initiation ceremony into the *Khalsa*, or Sikh brotherhood, is the most important religious event in their life.

The service was started in 1699 when the tenth guru, Guru Gobind Singh, called on five men to offer to give their lives for their religion. These five were the first members of the *Khalsa*, which means "the pure ones."

Today, people can become members of the *Khalsa* by taking part in the Sikh initiation ceremony, called *Amrit Sanskar,* or *Amrit Parchar.* Boys and girls of at least fourteen years of age can be initiated. They must have the five Ks of the Sikhs: *kesh*-uncut hair; *kangha*-comb; *kirpan*-sword; *kaccha*-short trousers; *kara*-steel bracelet.

The ceremony is usually held in a Sikh temple, but it can take place anywhere as long as the *Guru Granth Sahib*, the Sikh holy book

Sikhs representing the first members of the Khalsa *lead a procession.*

is present. Five members of the *Khalsa*, of either sex, conduct the ceremony. The main beliefs of the Sikhs are read aloud and each candidate is asked to accept them. *Amrit*, a

A Sikh reading a passage from the Guru Granth Sahib.

mixture of water and sugar pellets, is prepared. Each candidate says:

> *"Waheguru ji ka Khalsa, sri Waheguru ji ki Fateh."*

This means:

> *"The Khalsa is of God, the victory is to God."*

The candidates then drink a mouthful of the *amrit* and more is sprinkled on their eyes

Karah parshad is given to everyone present at the end of a service.

and hair. This acts like a baptism. All this is repeated five times.

After this there are prayers and the new members of the *Khalsa* are told that they are now children of Guru Gobind Singh and his wife Mata Sahib Kaur. All male Sikhs take the surname *Singh* ("lion"), and all women are called *Kaur* ("princess").

At the end of the service, *karah parshad*, sweet food, is given to everyone present to show that they are all members of one brotherhood.

Glossary

Amrit Sanskar (Amrit Parchar) Sikh initiation ceremony.

Bar Mitzvah Jewish initiation ceremony for boys.

Bat Mitzvah Jewish initiation ceremony for girls, celebrated by some Jewish groups.

Bishop A Christian clergyman in charge of many churches in one area.

Bismallah Indian Muslim ceremony, during which children begin their religious instruction.

Buddha The founder of Buddhism.

Confirmation Christian initiation ceremony.

Dharma The teachings of Buddhism.

Guru A teacher, especially in India.

Hebrew The ancient language of the Jews.

Initiation Literally "a beginning"; a ceremony that admits a person into full membership of a religion, society, etc.

Initiate A person who is initiated.

Khalsa The brotherhood of Sikhs.

Mitzvot The commandments of the Jewish religion.

Muslims Followers of the religion of Islam.

Qur'an The Muslim holy book.

Rabbi A Jewish minister.

Synagogue Jewish place of worship.

Upanayana Hindu initiation ceremony.

Further Information

If you would like to find out more about the various religions discussed in this book, you may wish to read the following series:

Eastern Religions by Elizabeth Seeger. Published by Crowell Jr. Bks.

Founders of Religion by Tony D. Triggs. Published by Silver Burdett Co.

Religions by James Haskins. Published by Lippincott Junior Bks. Group.

Six World Religions by L. Aletrino. Published by Morehouse-Barlow Co.

Videos

Church Collection – helps to explain the role of the Protestant church in modern times. Includes the sacraments of Baptism and Holy Communion. 73 min. Produced by Family Films.

The Holy Koran – Islam's contributions to the world are examined. 60 min. Produced by Mastervision.

Holy Land and Holy City – a look at the Holy Land at Christmas and the activities of the Vatican during the reign of Pope Paul VI. 58 min. Produced by Mastervision.

The Message – the life of Muhammad, founder of the Islamic religion. 180 min. Produced by USA.

Acknowlegments

The publisher would like to thank all those who provided pictures on the following pages: Camerapix 5, 8, 26, 27; Bruce Coleman Ltd 24, 25; Hutchison Library *cover*, 7, 9, 15; Sally and Richard Greenhill 10, 11, 19, 28, 29; Ann and Bury Peerless 10, 18; Sri Lanka Tourist Board 6; United Society for the Propagation of the Gospel 12; ZEFA 4, 5, 13, 14, 20, 21, 23.

Index